The Jerk Ways

Phenomenal Swear Word To Color

For Stress Releasing

J.N. Moorcroft

Happy Coloring!

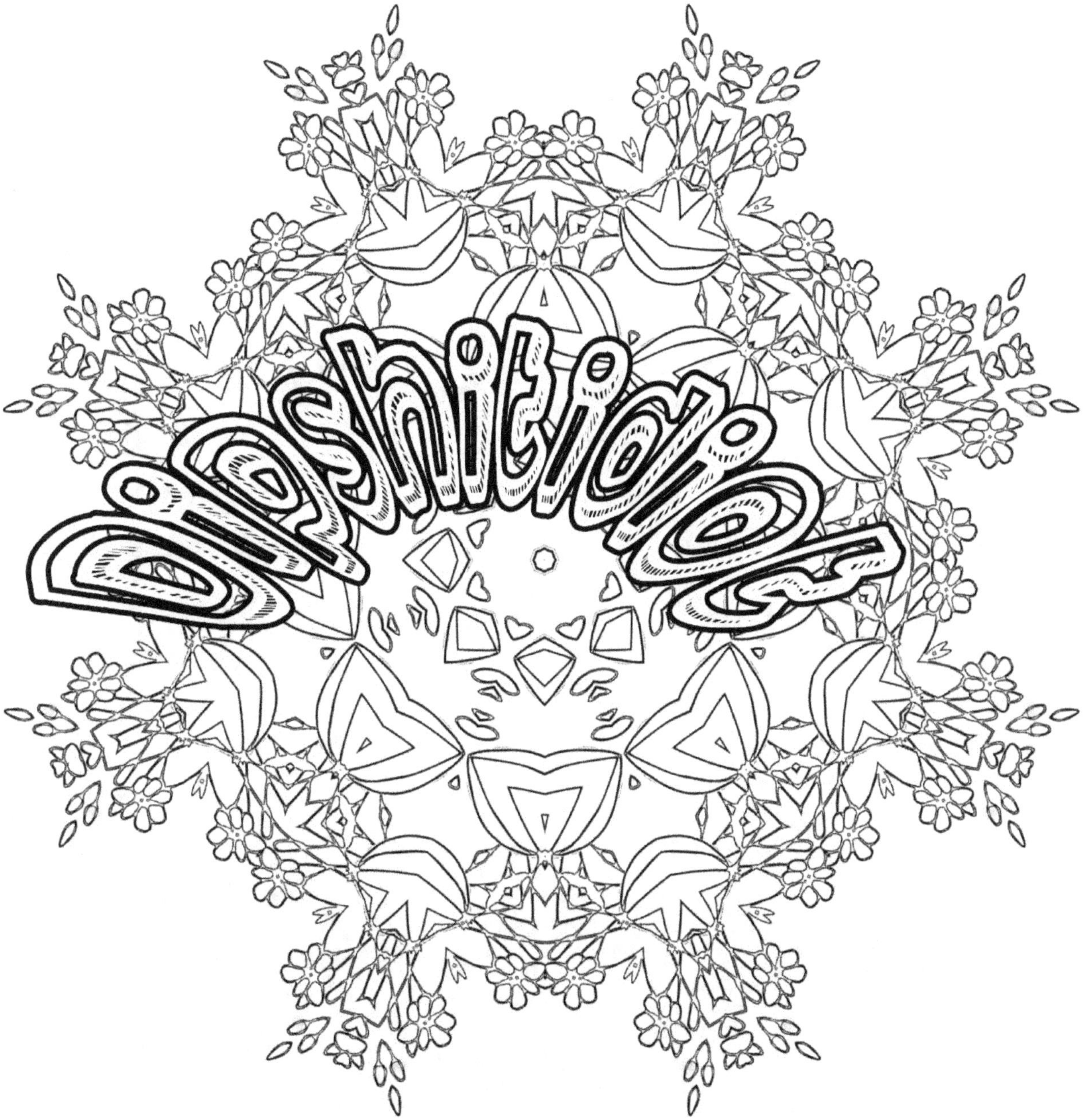

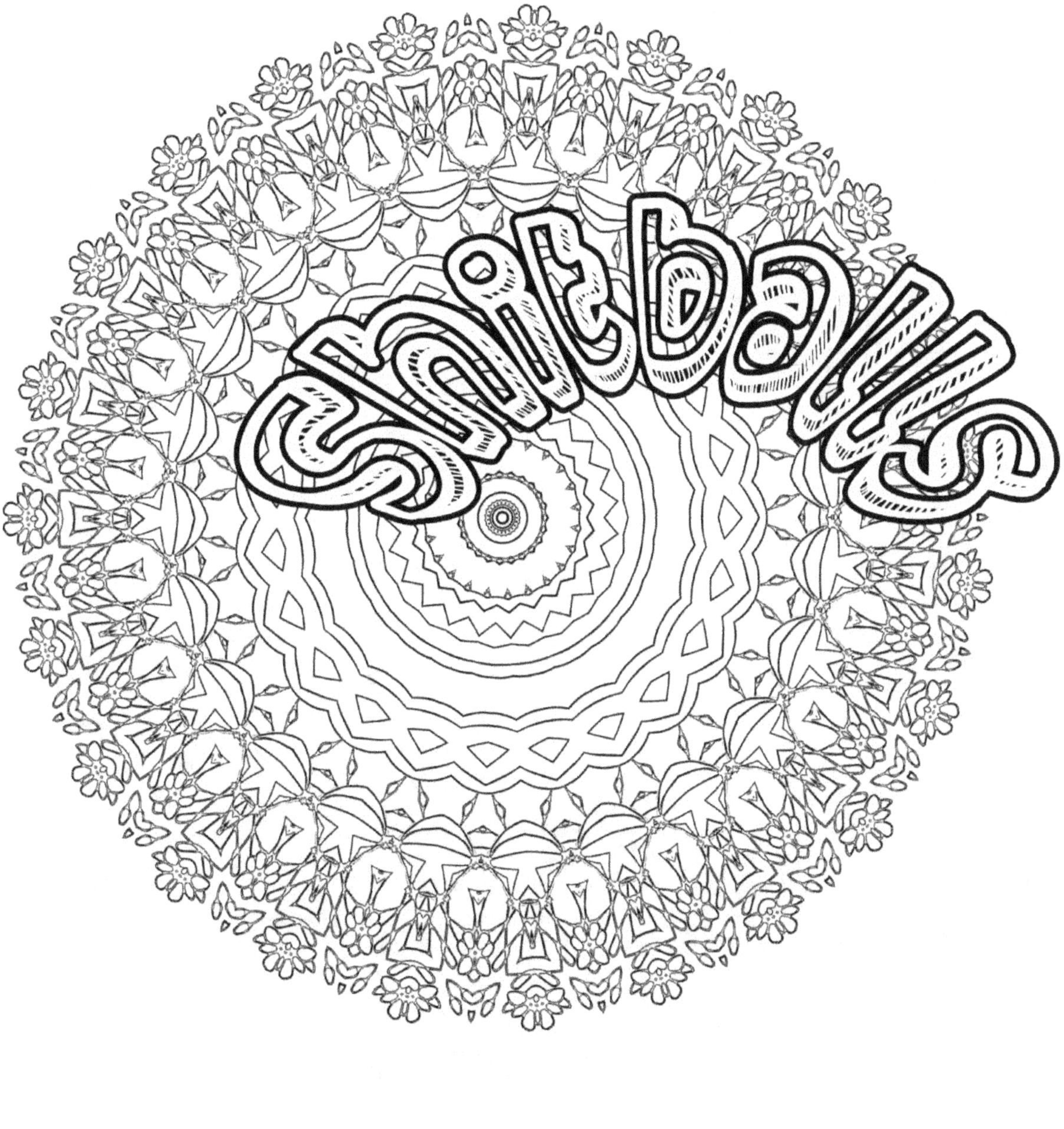
shitballs

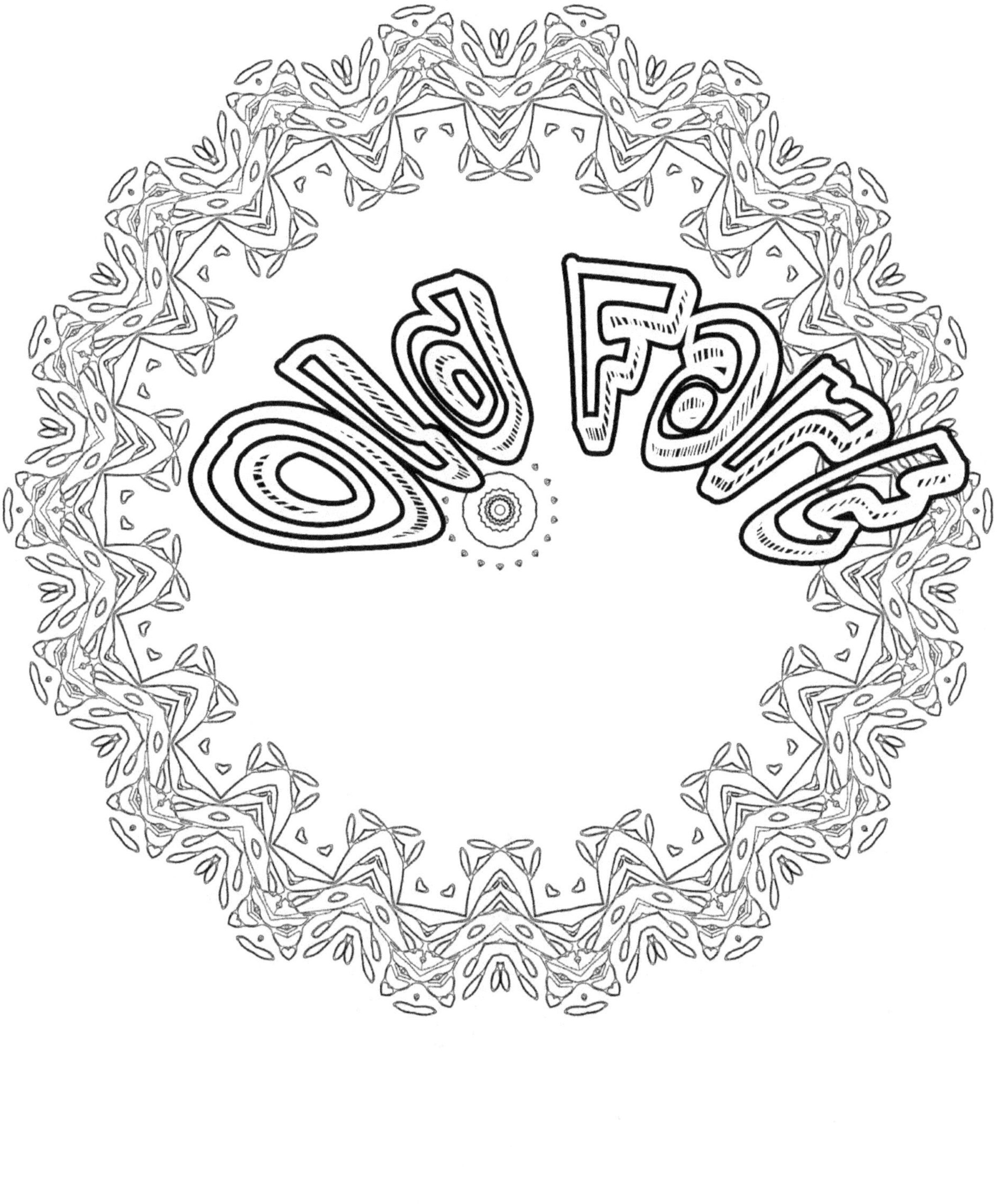
Old Farts

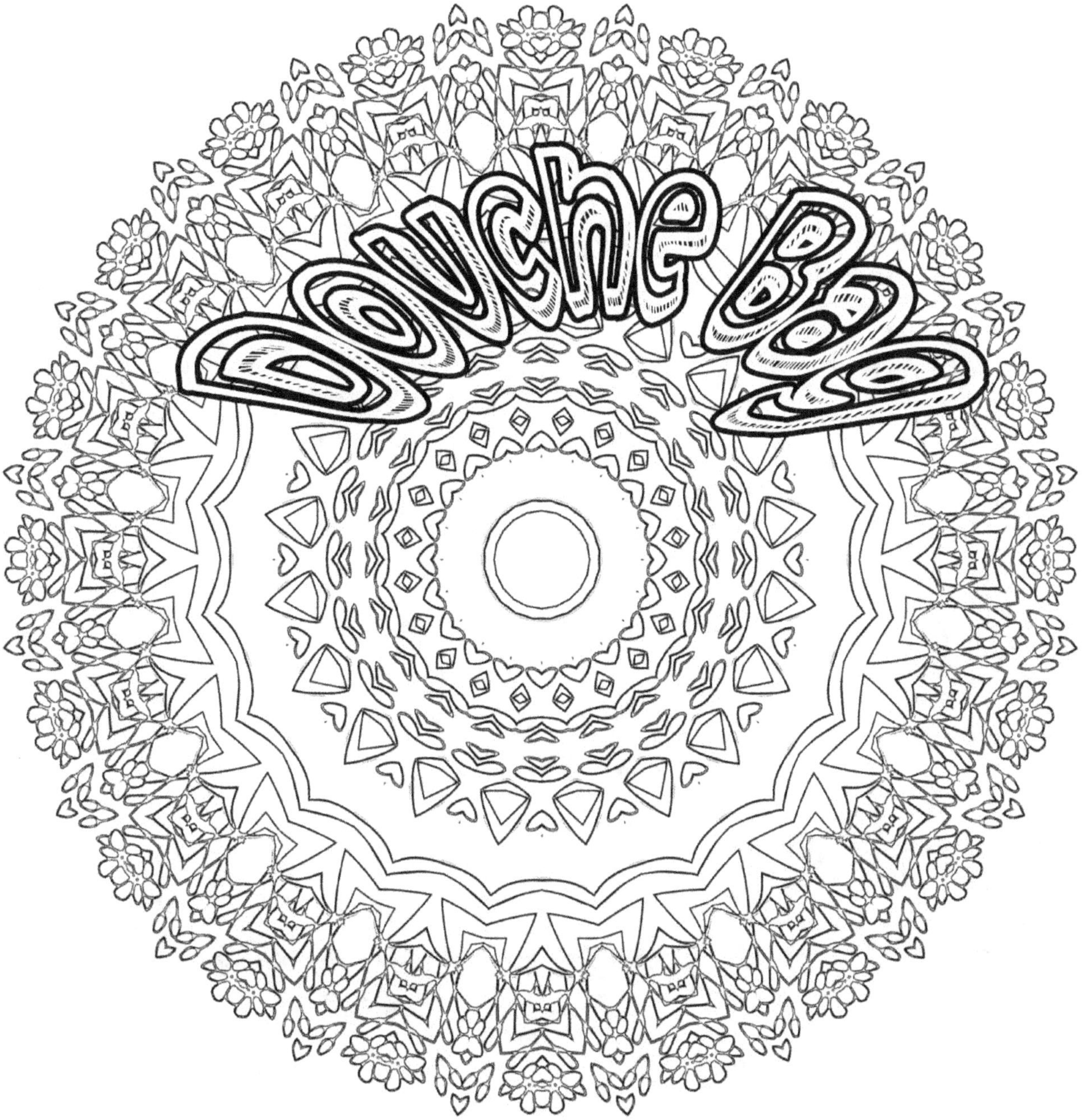
Douche Bag

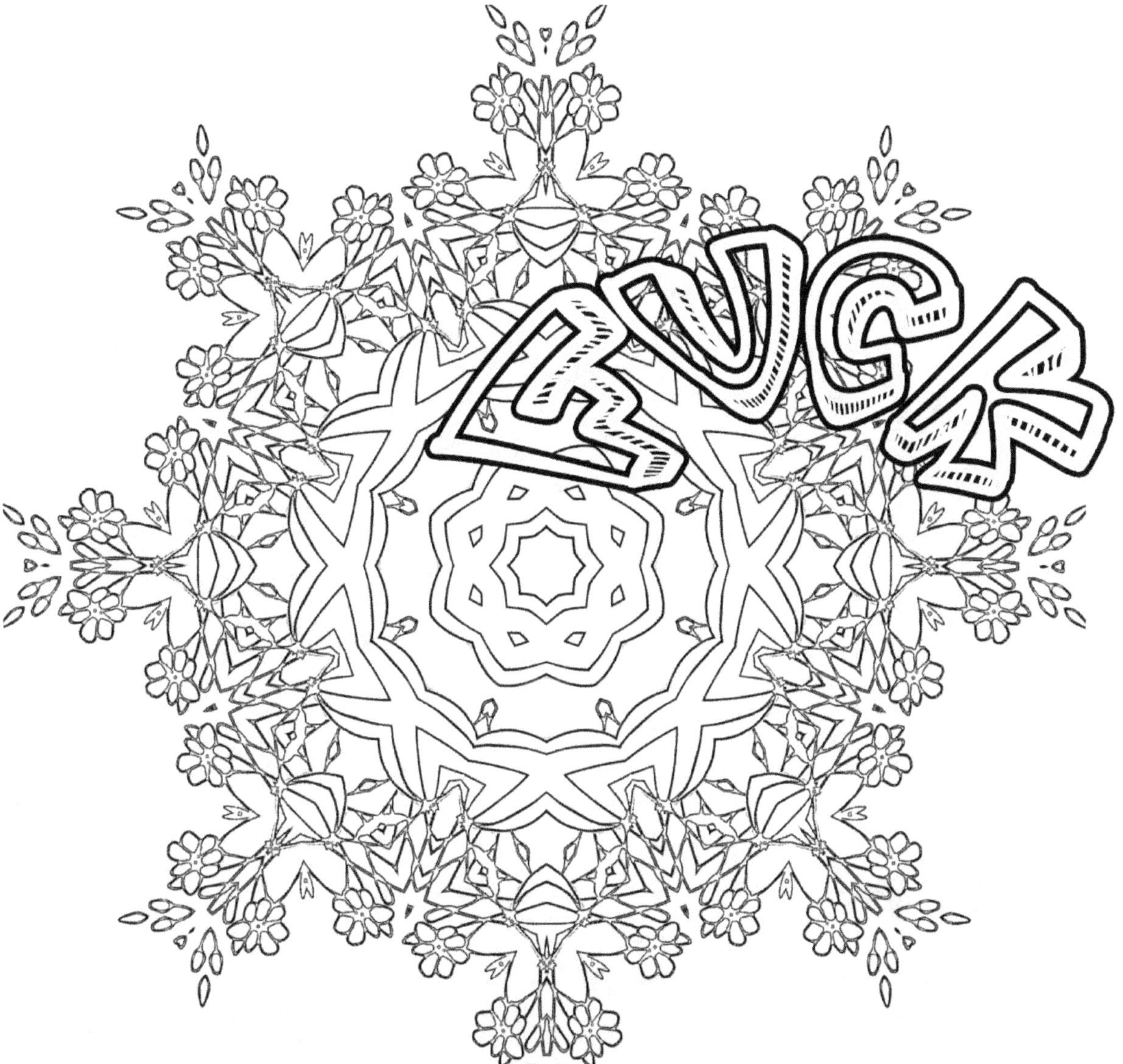
FUCK

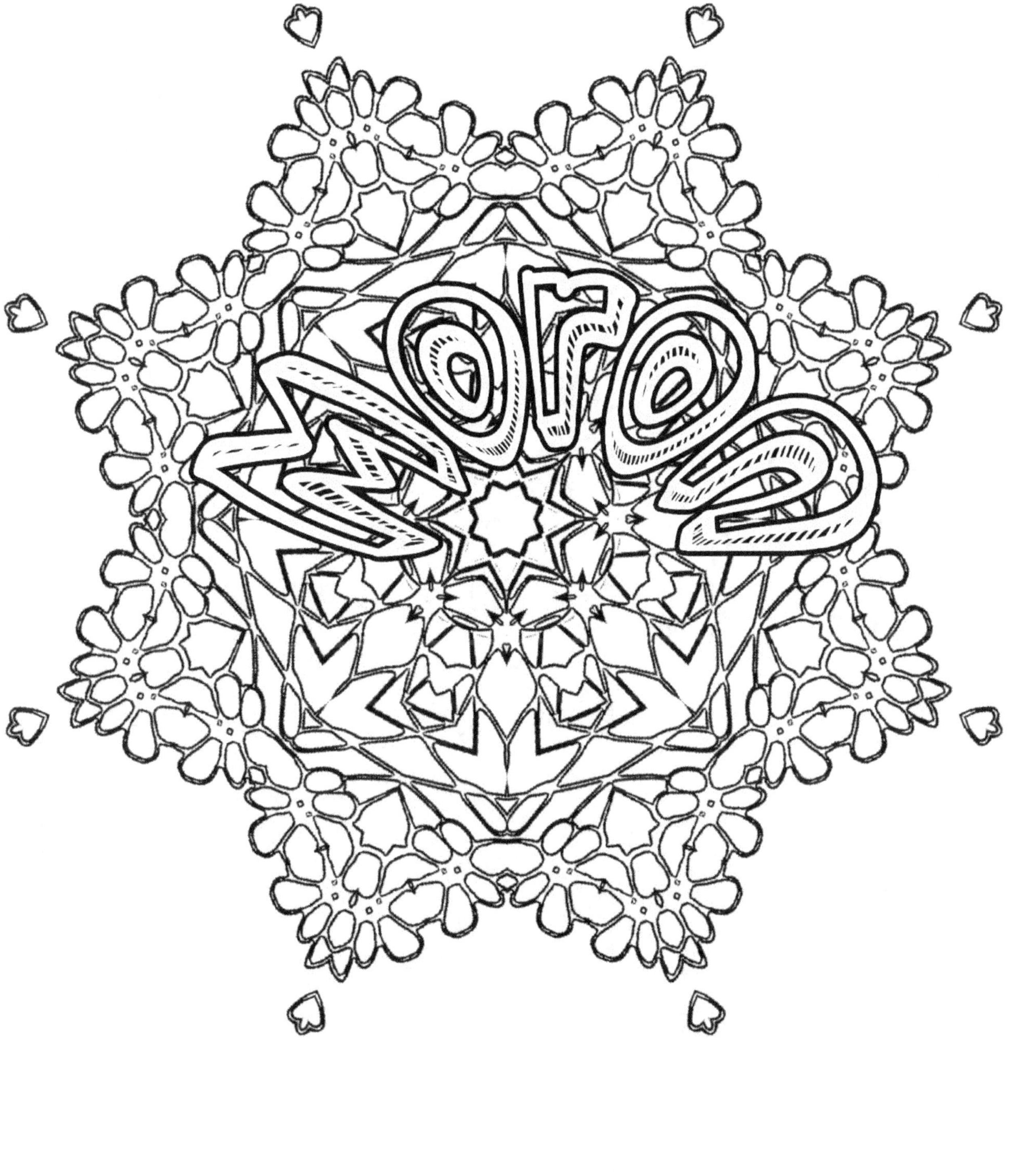

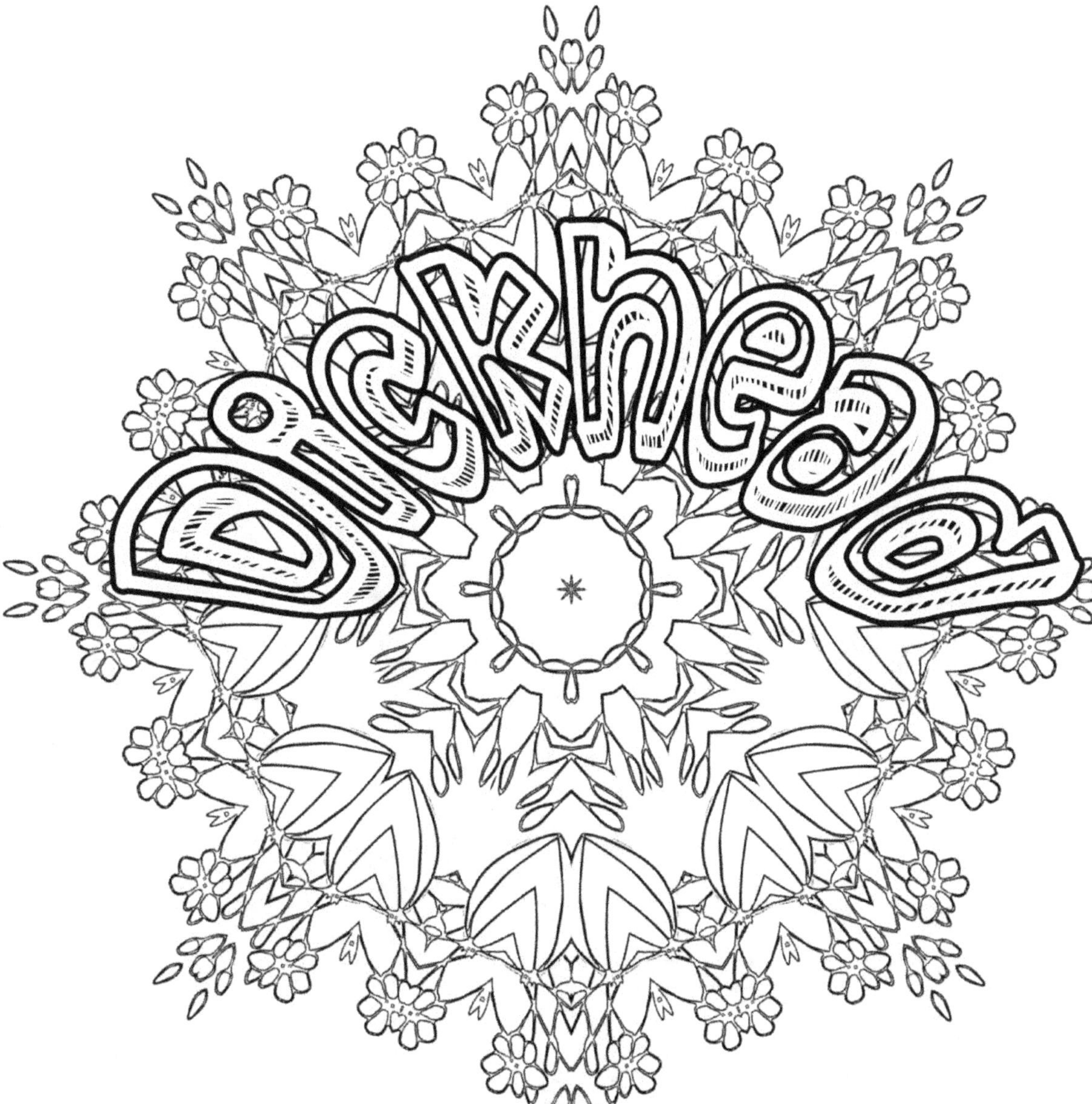
Dickhead

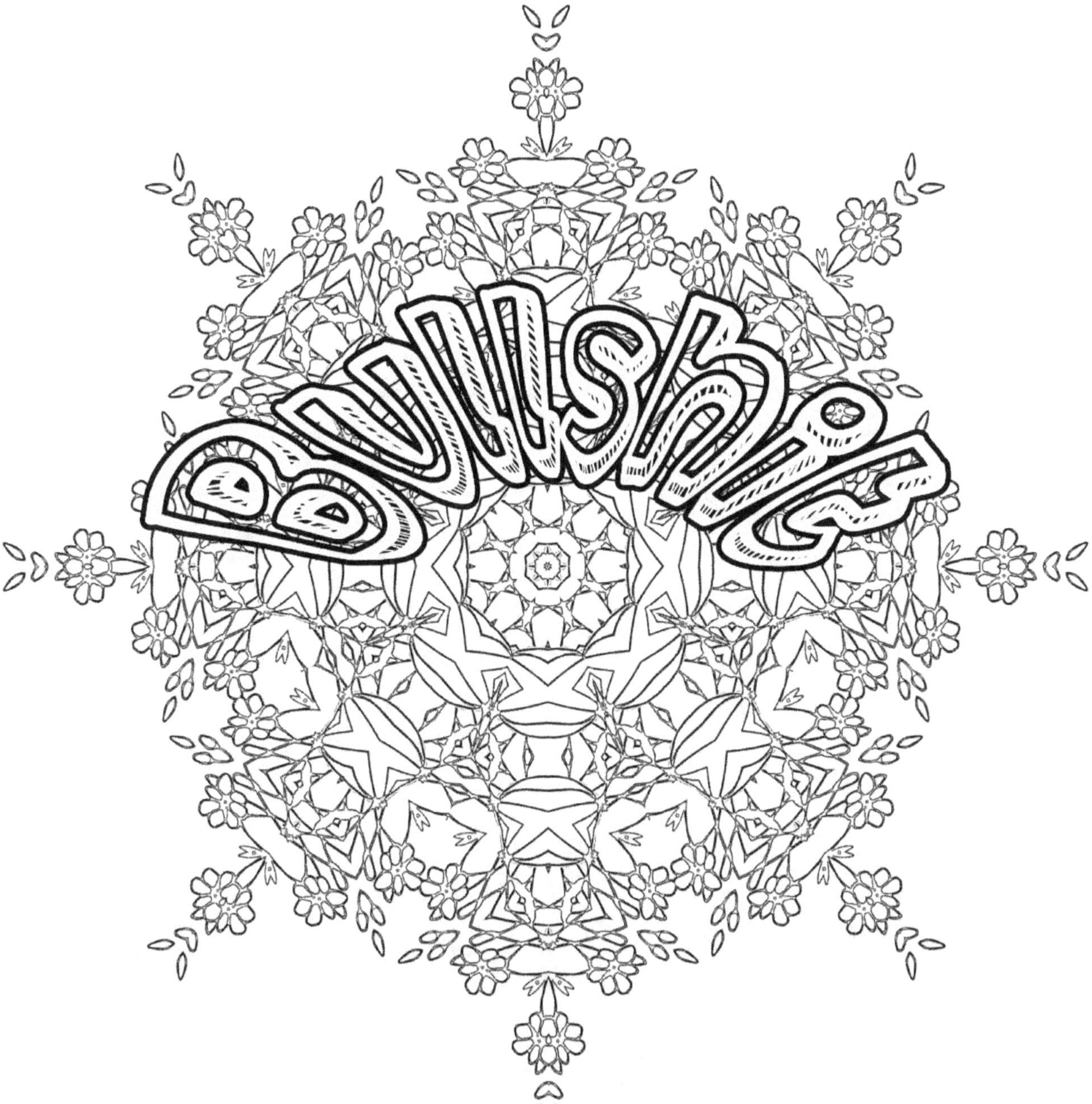

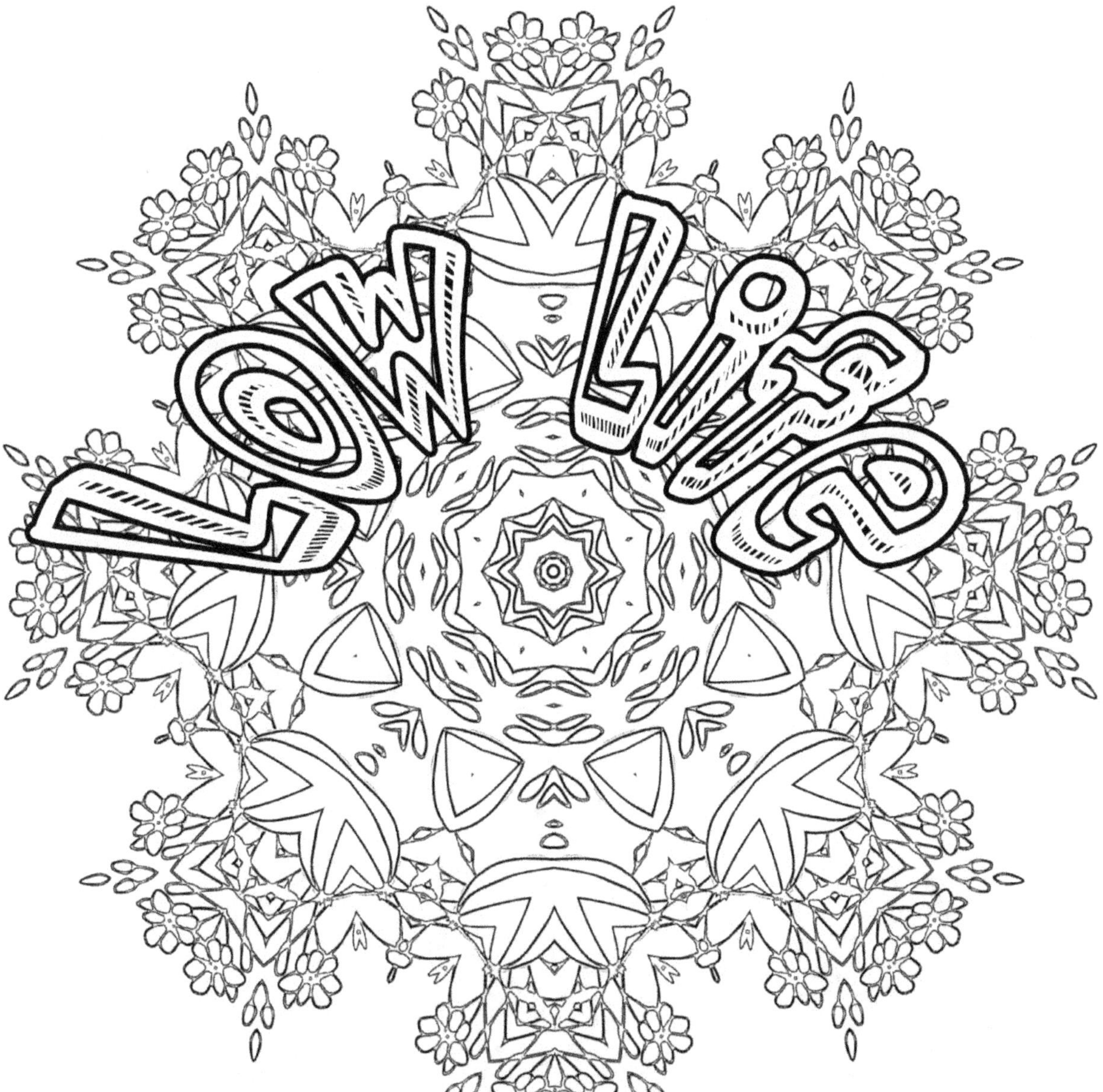
Low Life

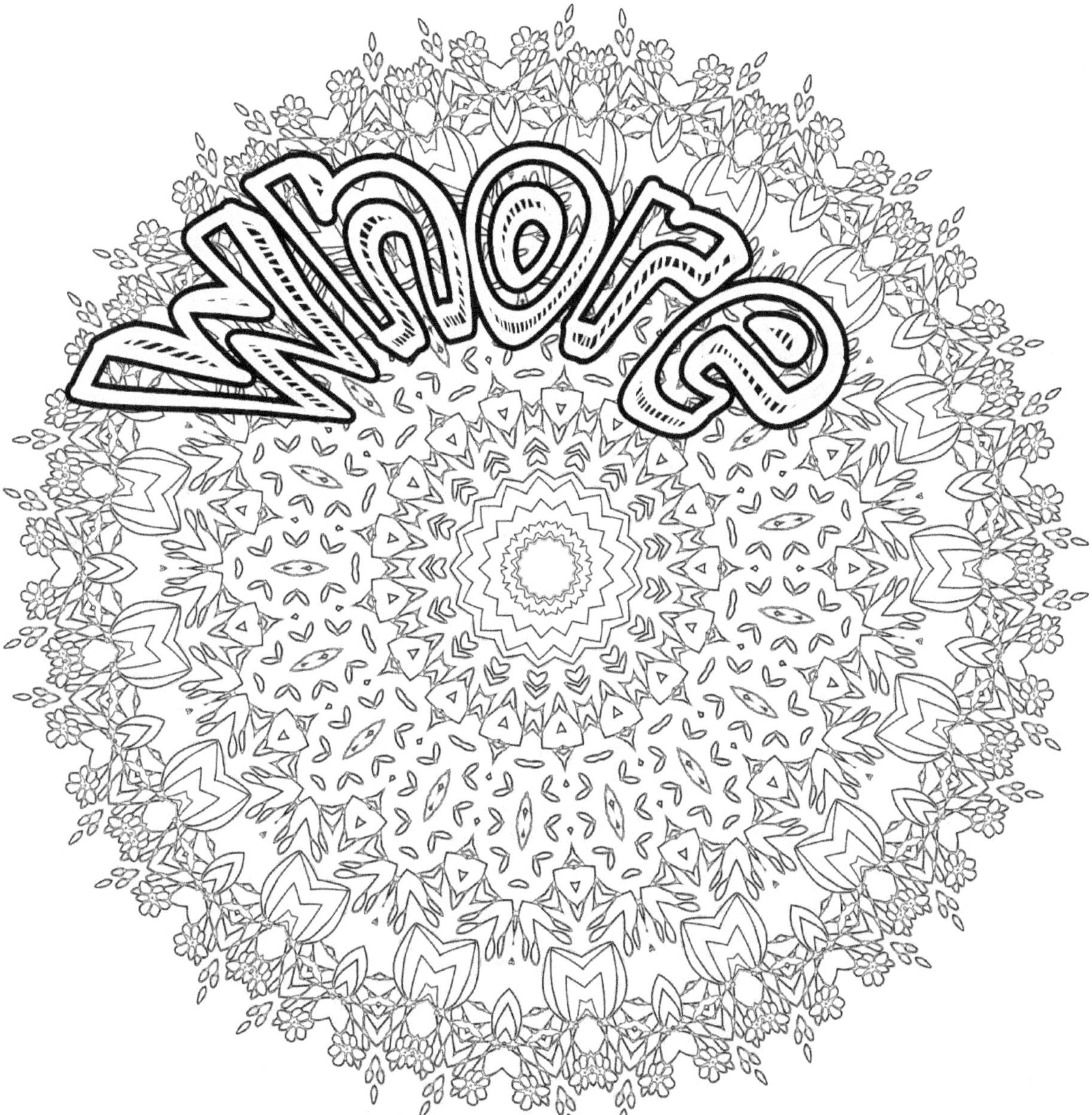
whore

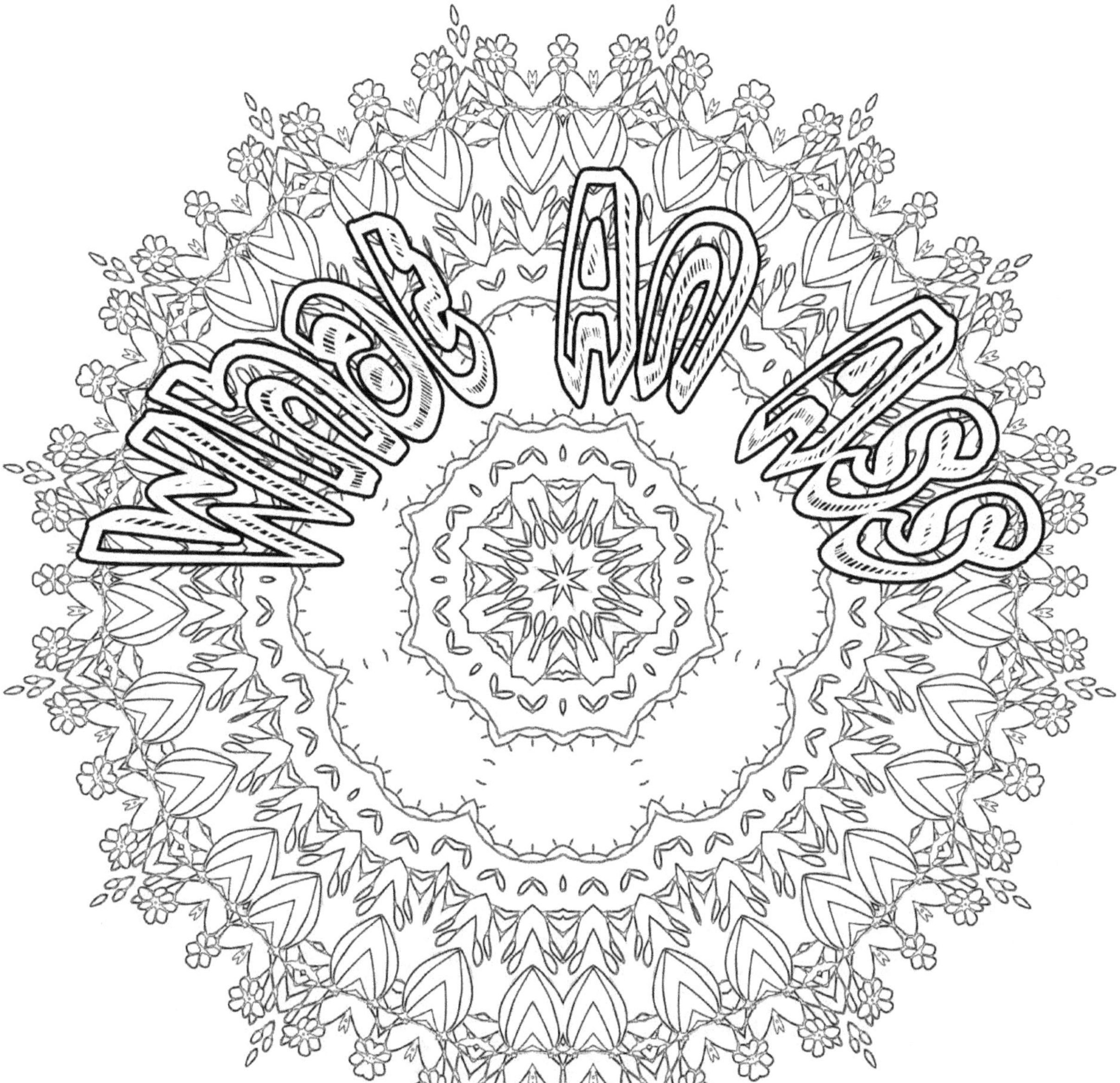
What An Ass

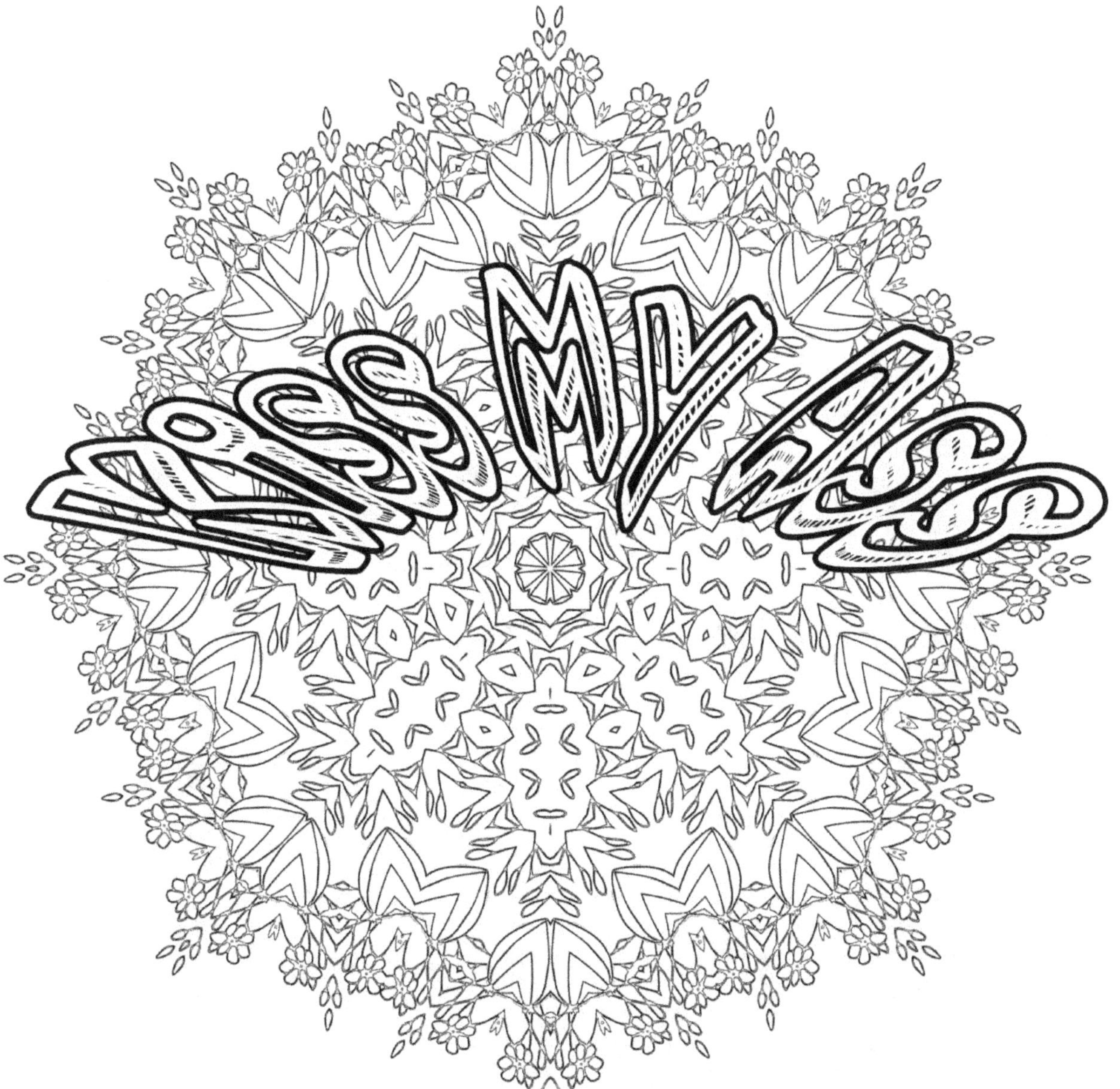
KISS MY ASS

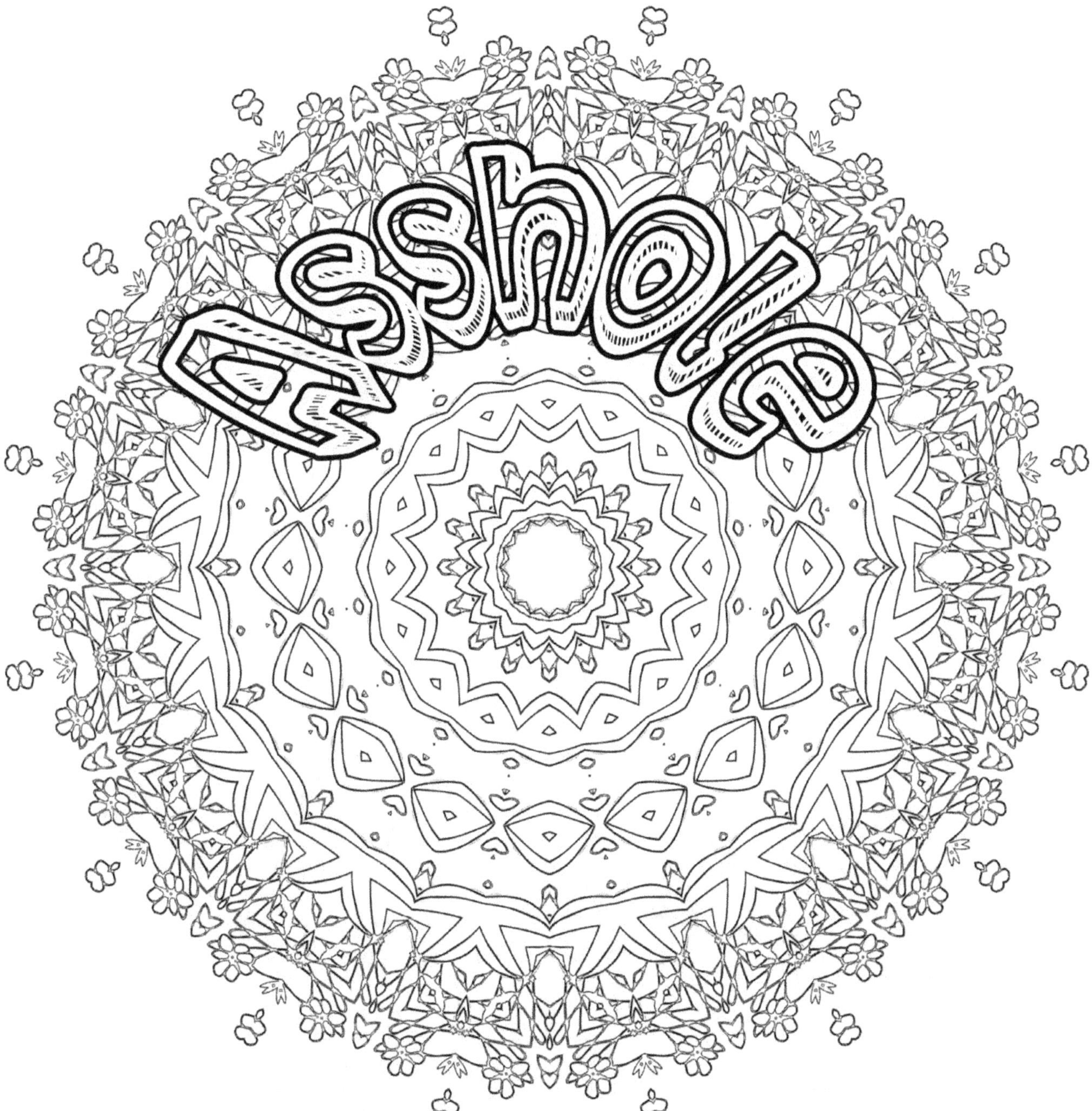
Asshole

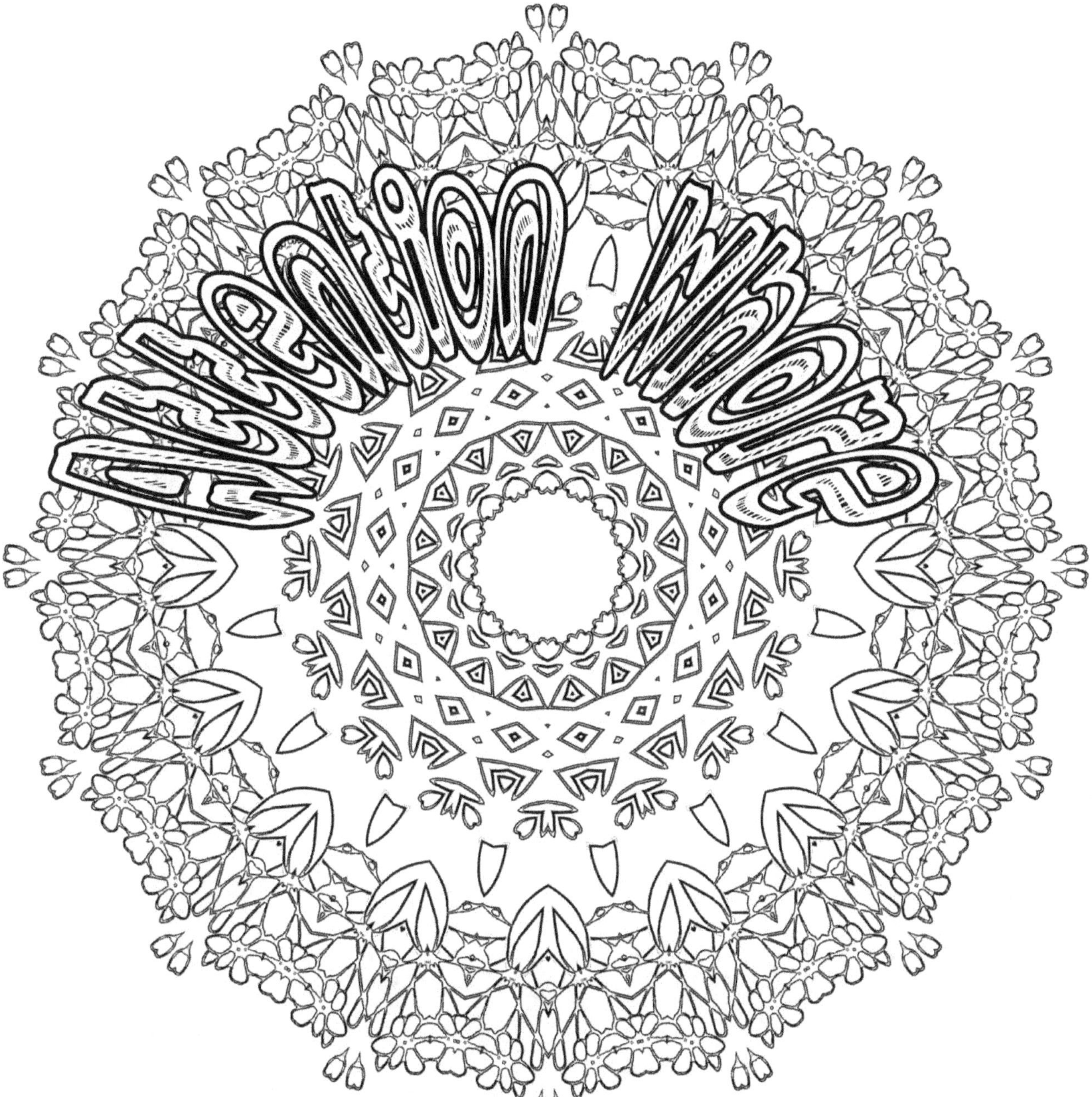
Attention More

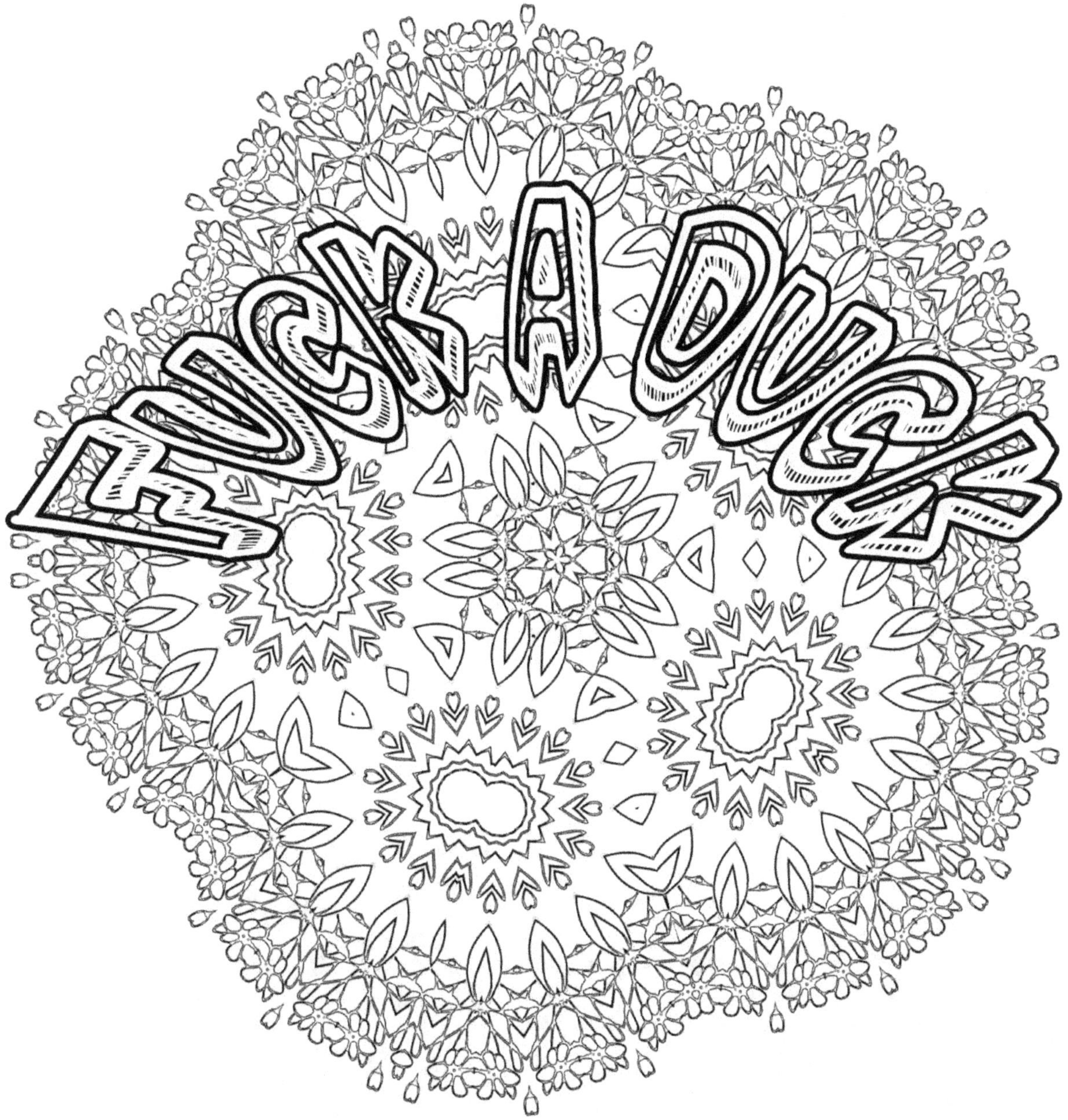
FUCK A DUCK

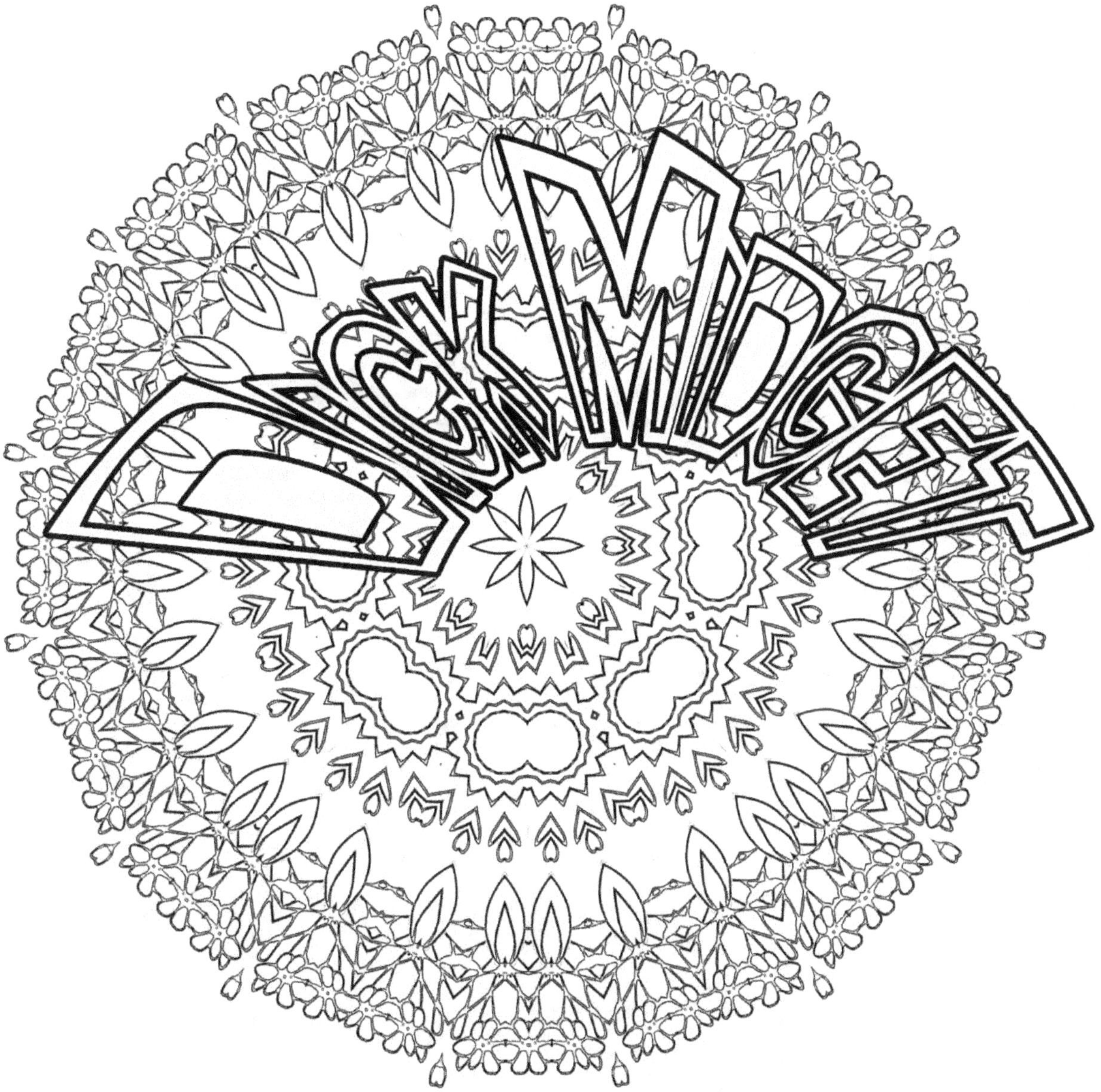

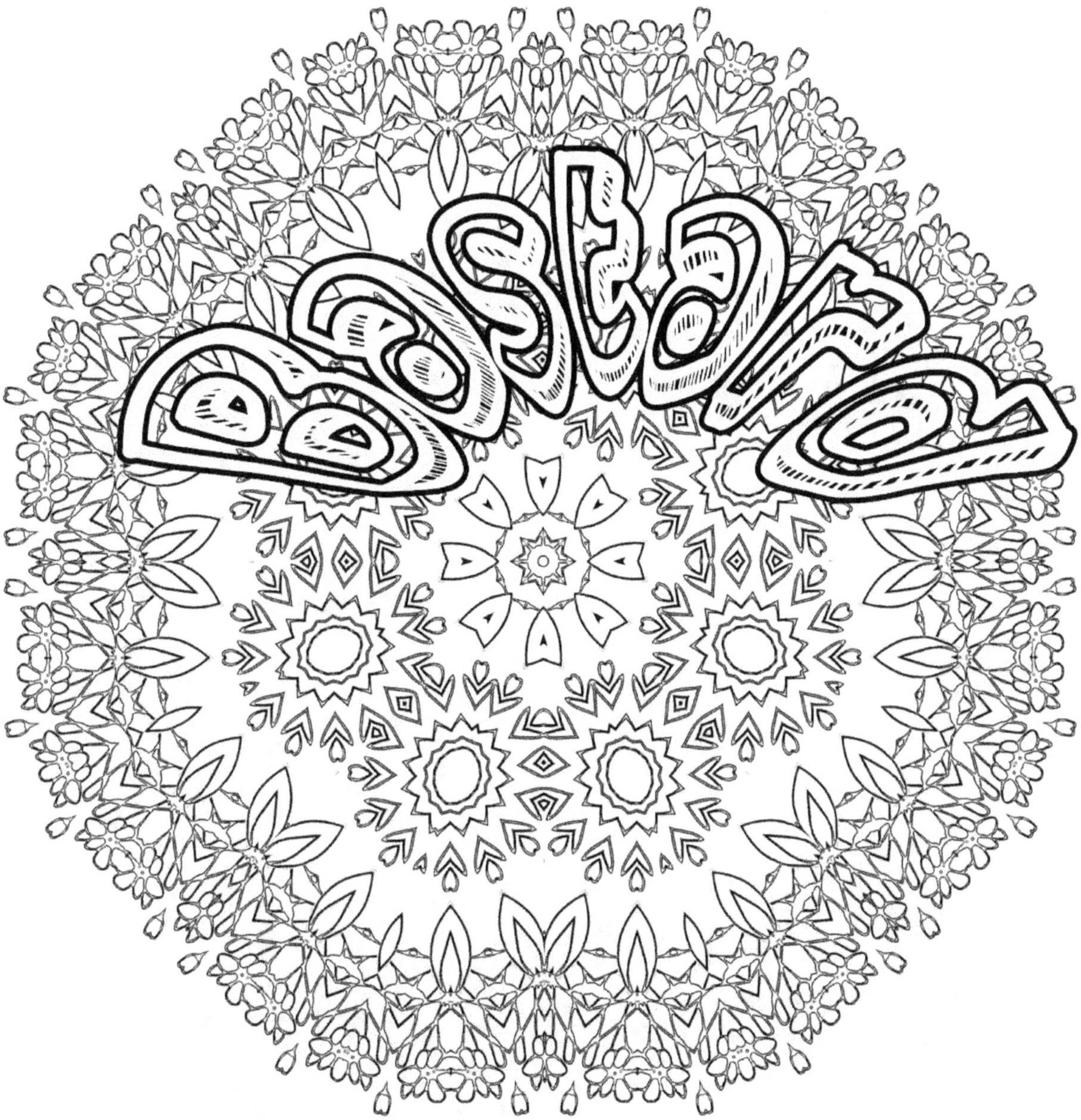
Bastard

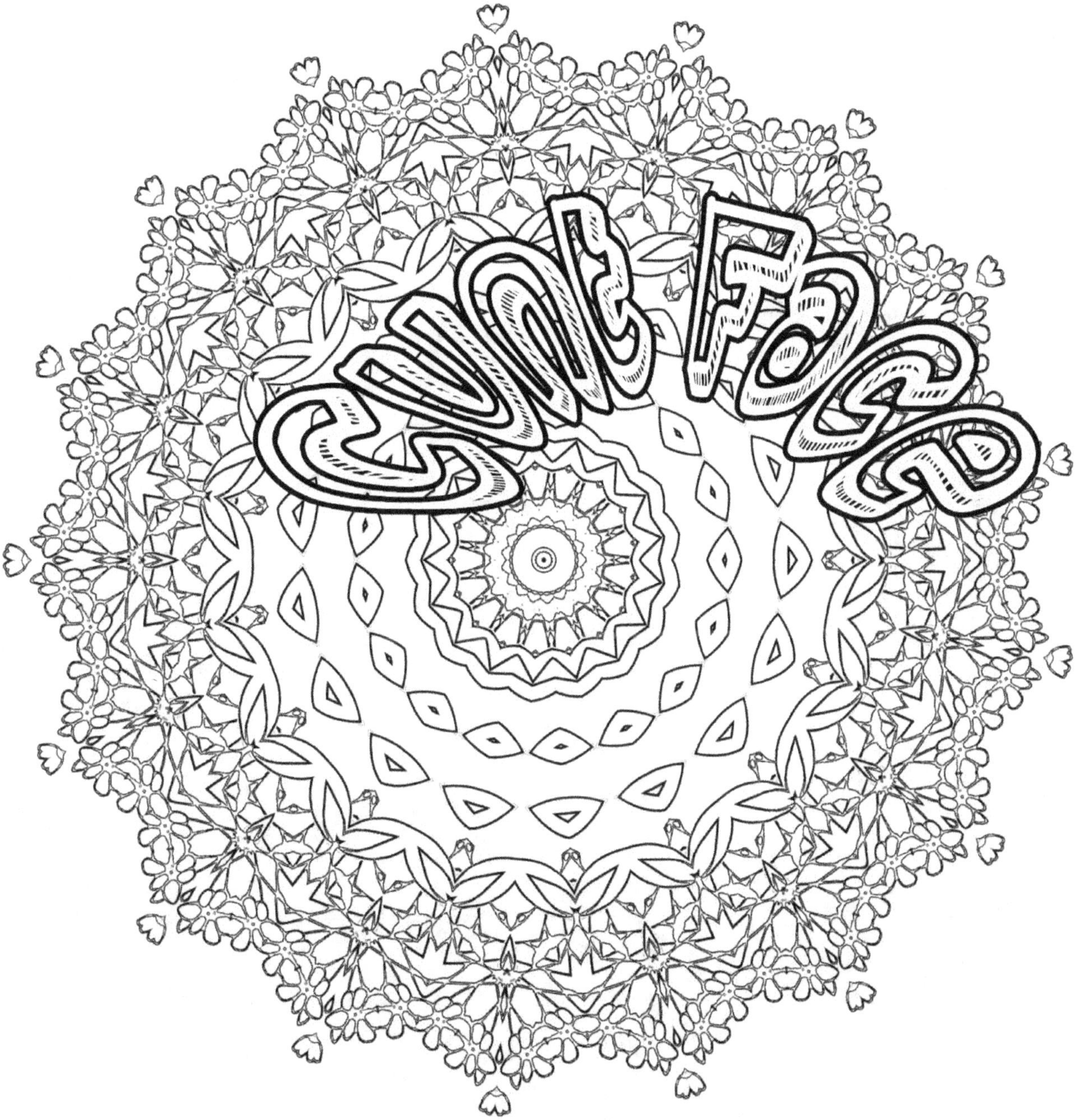
Cunt Face

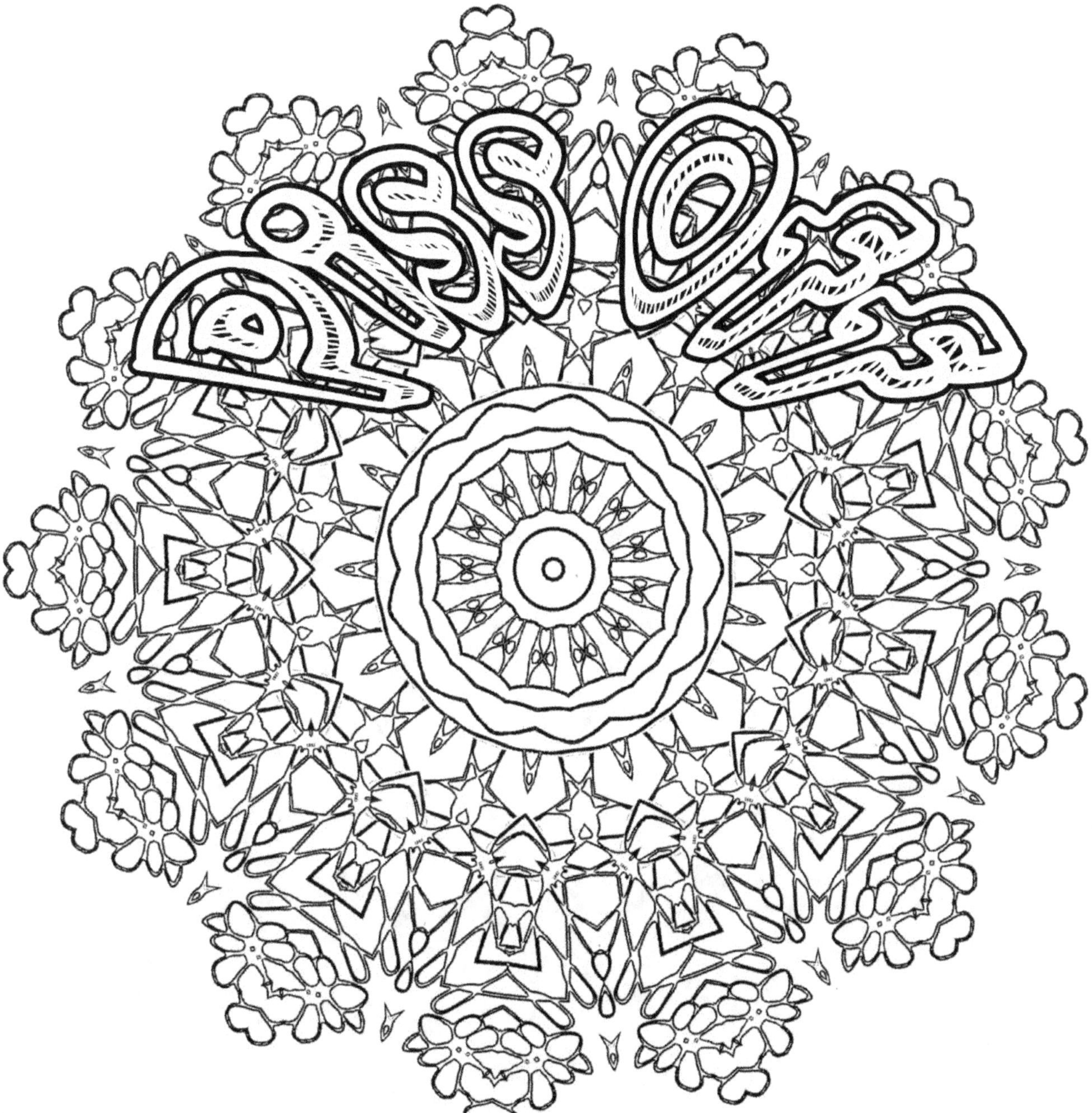

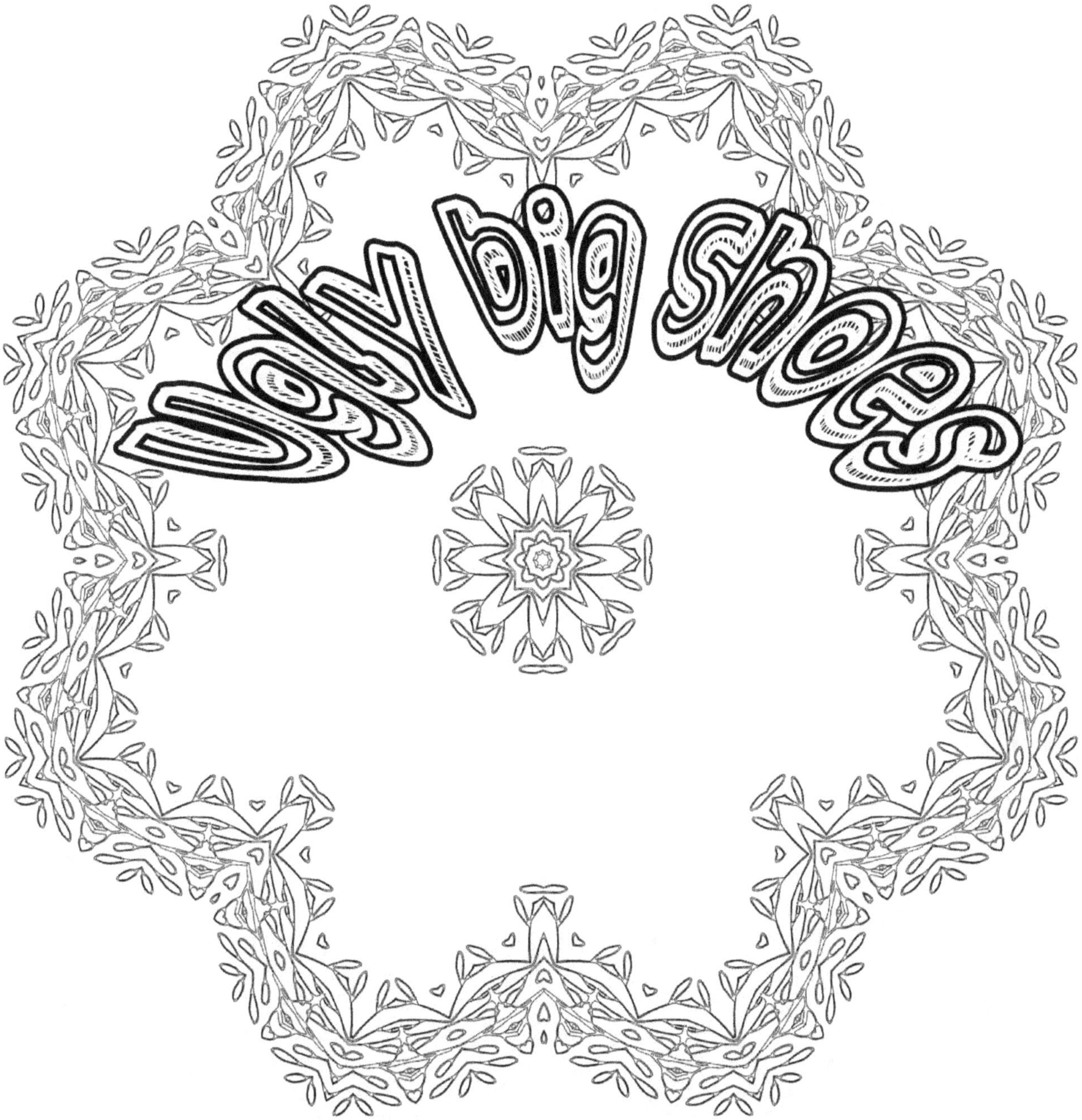
Ugly big shoes

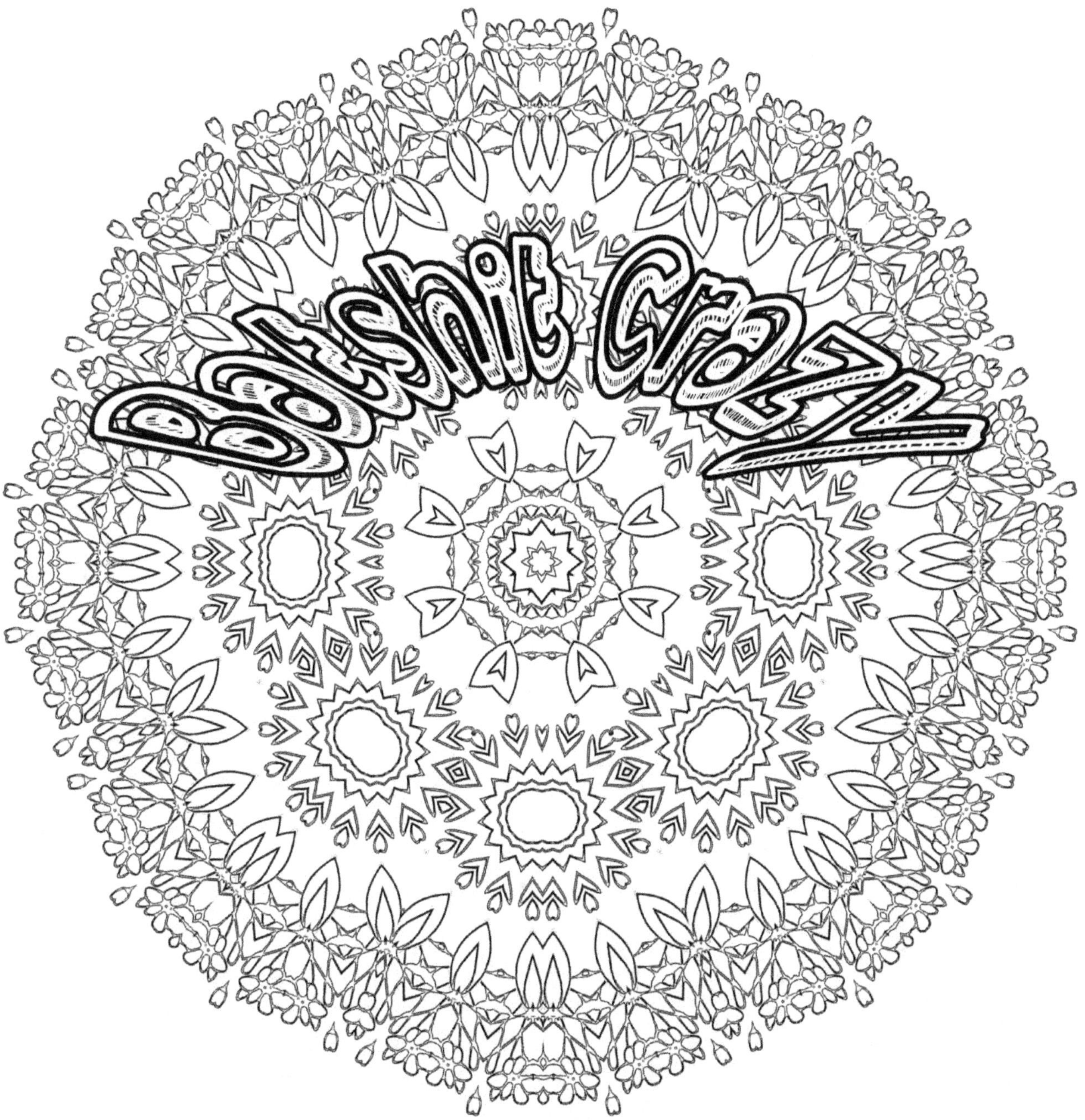
Batshit Crazy

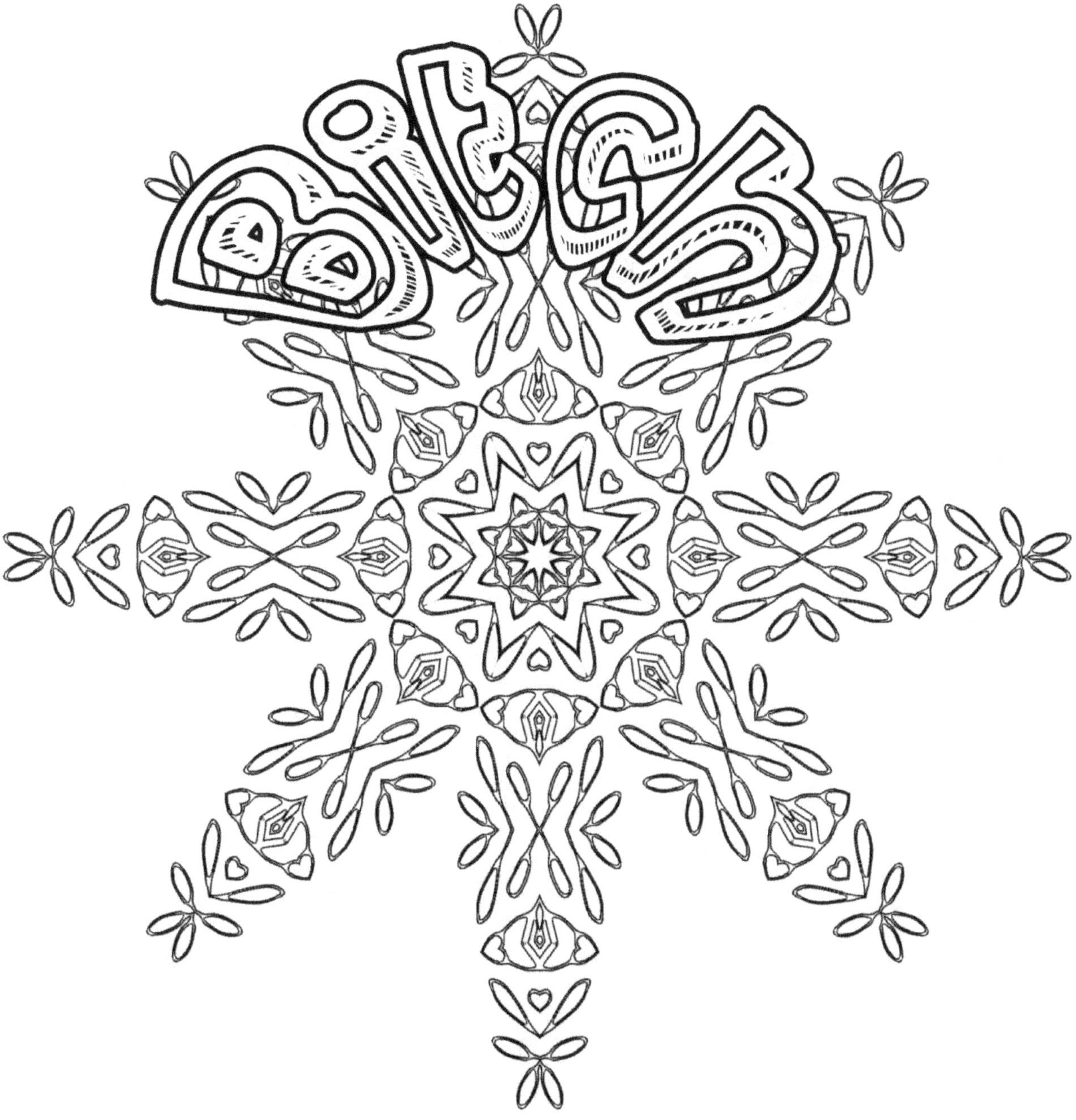
Bitch

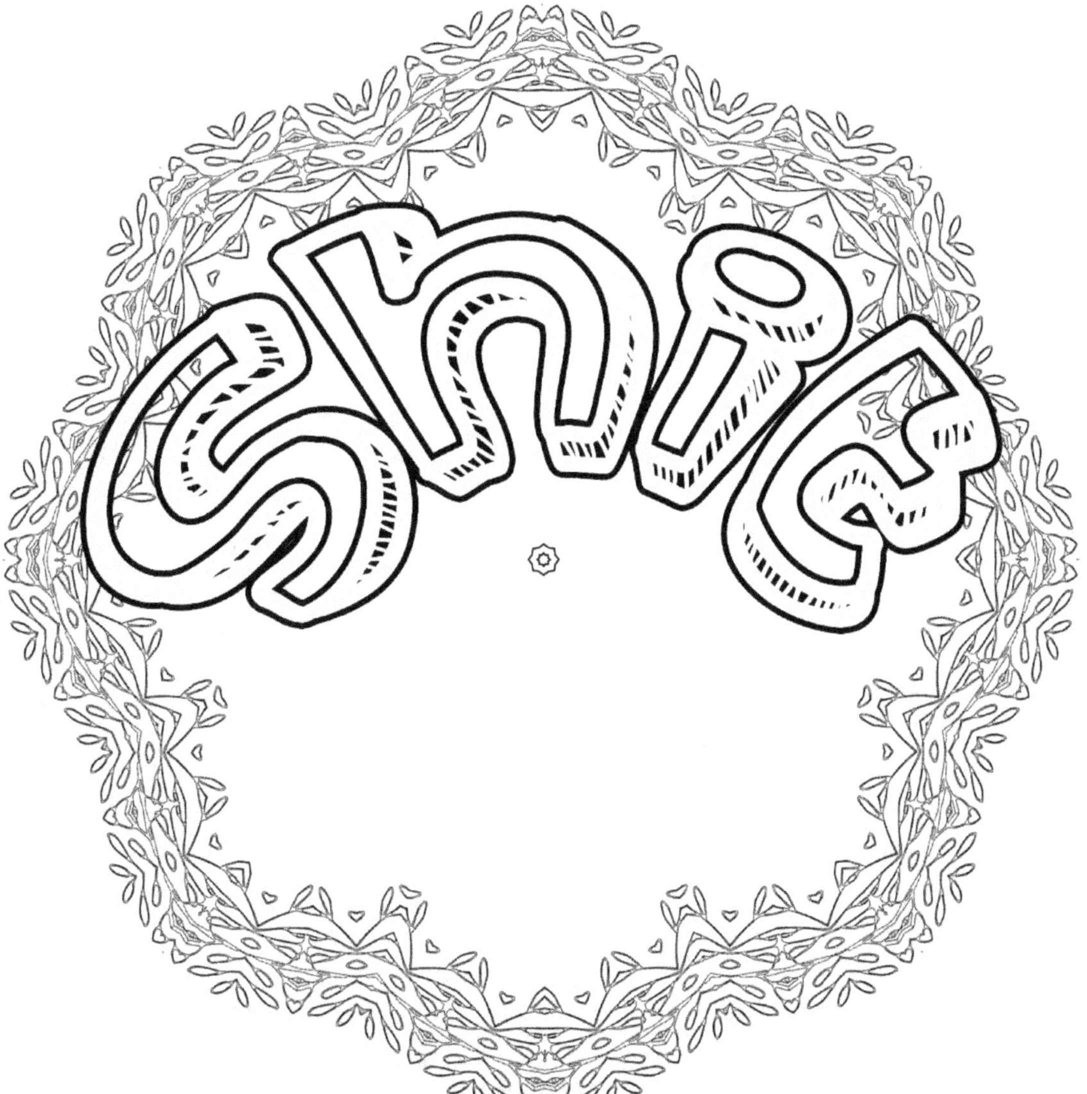
Chic

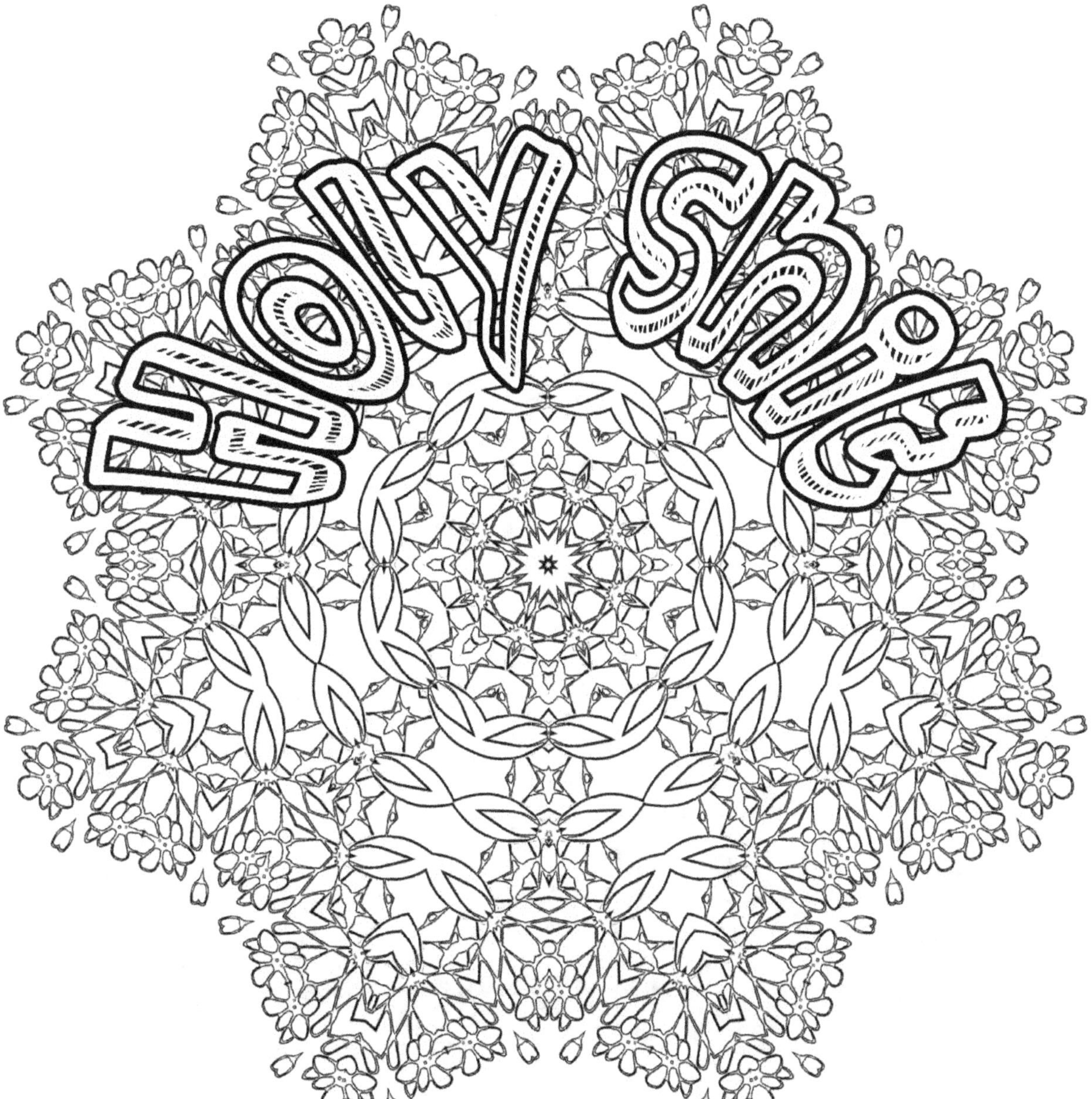
Holy Shit

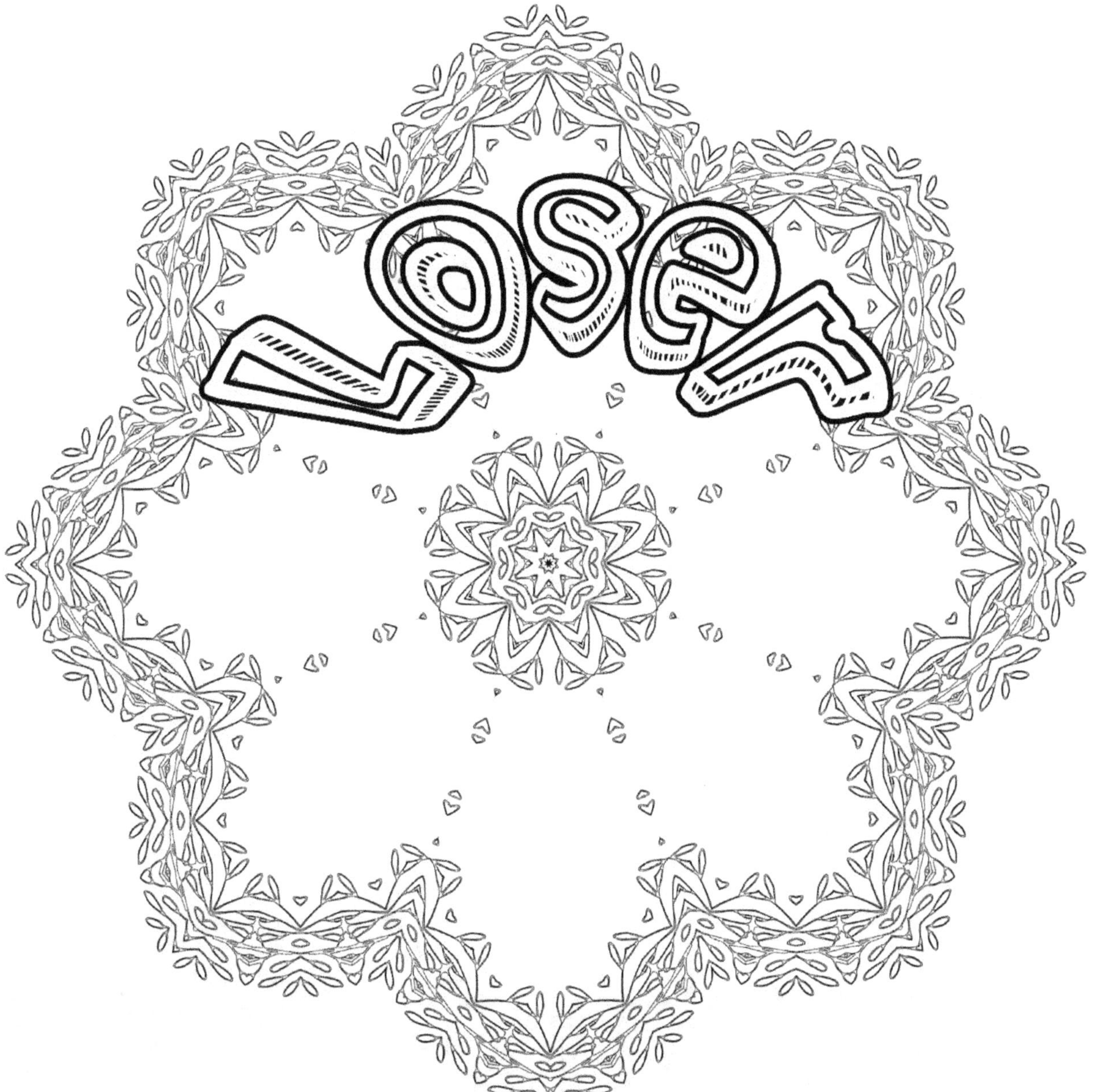
Loser

www.ingramcontent.com/pod-product-compliance
Lightning Source LLC
Chambersburg PA
CBHW081750170526
45167CB00009B/3982
* 9 7 8 1 5 4 4 1 8 1 0 4 2 *